Take Off! All About Airplanes

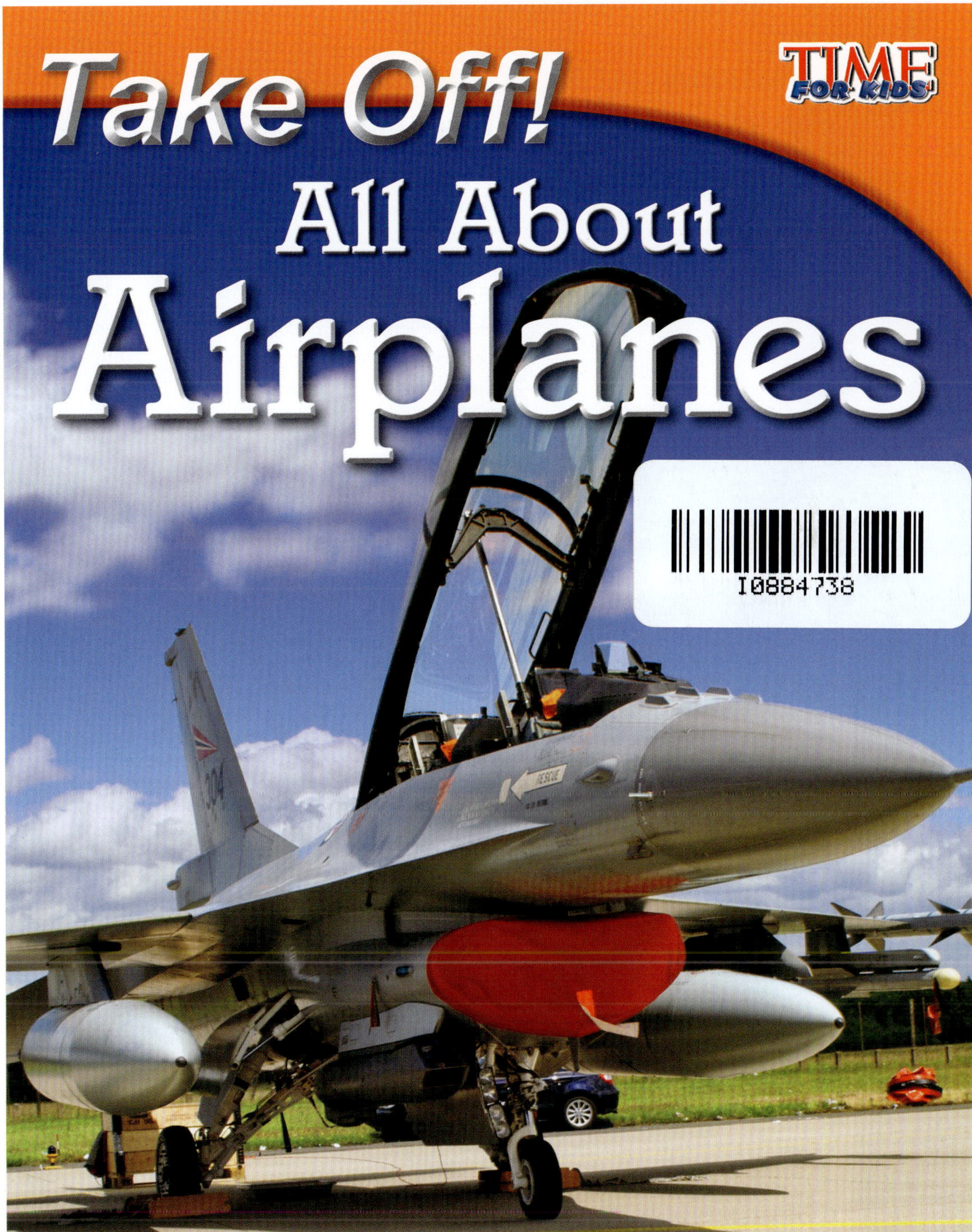

Jennifer Prior

Consultants

Timothy Rasinski, Ph.D.
Kent State University

Alan J. Cross,
Automotive Engineer

John Goldfluss,
Pilot

Publishing Credits

Dona Herweck Rice, *Editor-in-Chief*
Robin Erickson, *Production Director*
Lee Aucoin, *Creative Director*
Conni Medina, M.A.Ed., *Editorial Director*
Jamey Acosta, *Editor*
Heidi Kellenberger, *Editor*
Lexa Hoang, *Designer*
Stephanie Reid, *Photo Editor*
Rachelle Cracchiolo, M.S.Ed., *Publisher*

Image Credits

Cover ssuaphotos/Shutterstock; p.3 Samuel Acosta/Shutterstock; p.4 Karen Hadley/Shutterstock; p.5 top to bottom: Sylvie Bouchard/Shutterstock; Elena Elisseeva/Shutterstock; p.6 left to right: Getty Images; Mechanics' Magazine vol. 57, 1852 via Google Books; LOC-LC-USZ62-100556; p.7 top to bottom: Canicula/Shutterstock; Johan Swanepoel/Shutterstock; p.7 left to right: LOC-LC-USZ62-6166A; LOC-LC-USZ62-15783; LOC-LC-USZ62-94567; p.8 left to right: LOC-LC-DIG-ppmsc-0610; LOC-LC-DIG-pppr s-00683; p.9 LOC-LC-USZ62-6166A; p.10-11 LOC-LC-USZ62-108514; p.10 LOC-LC-DIG-ggbain-35317; p.11 LOC-LC-USZ62-45002; p.12 Kamira/Shutterstock; p12-13 Jacques Rouchon/akg-images/Newscom; p.13 Mirrorpix/Newscom; p.15 iPhotos/Shutterstock; p.16 Ilja Mašík/Shutterstock; p.17 top to bottom: Vibrant Image Studio/Shutterstock; Carlos E. Santa Maria/Shutterstock; p.18 Peteri/Shutterstock; p.19 top to bottom: ssuaphotos/Shutterstock; yuyangc/Shutterstock; p.20 Denis Barbulat/Shutterstock; p.21 top to bottom: Carlos E. Santa Maria/Shutterstock; p.21 Paul Matthew Photography/Shutterstock; p.22 AFP/Getty Images; p.23 Inara Prusakova/Shutterstock; p.24 sjlocke/iStockphoto; p.25 top to bottom: withGod/Shutterstock; photobank.chShutterstock; p.26 Demid Borodin/Shutterstock; p.26 inset: 3DDock/Shutterstock; p.28 Kamira/Shutterstock; background: alekup/Shutterstock; back cover: J van der Wolf/Shutterstock

Based on writing from *TIME For Kids.*

Teacher Created Materials
5301 Oceanus Drive
Huntington Beach, CA 92649-1030
http://www.tcmpub.com

ISBN 978-1-4333-3655-3

Printed by: 590835
Printed in: China

Table of Contents

Airplane

Airplane, airplane, up so high,
Flying through the clear blue sky,
Floating on the gentle breeze,
Soaring, soaring, with such ease.

1910 Bristol kite wing replica ▲

Over 700 million people fly in the United States every year.

A Brief History of Planes

Have you ever watched a bird and wished you could fly? It seems people have always dreamed of flying. In fact, as early as the 1800s, people tried to make flying machines.

So, what would be a good **model** for a plane? You might think a bird's body would be the best model. Many people tried this. However, machines made in this way did not work.

What Is It?

Model is a word with many meanings. Here, it means an object that is used as a plan for something else that will be built.

Flight Time Line

November 21, 1783

Jacques Alexandre César Charles and M.N. Robert fly in the first hydrogen balloon.

1853

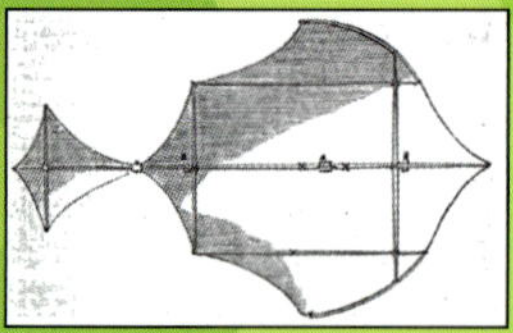

The first George Cayley glider is flown.

July 2, 1900

The first zeppelin is flown

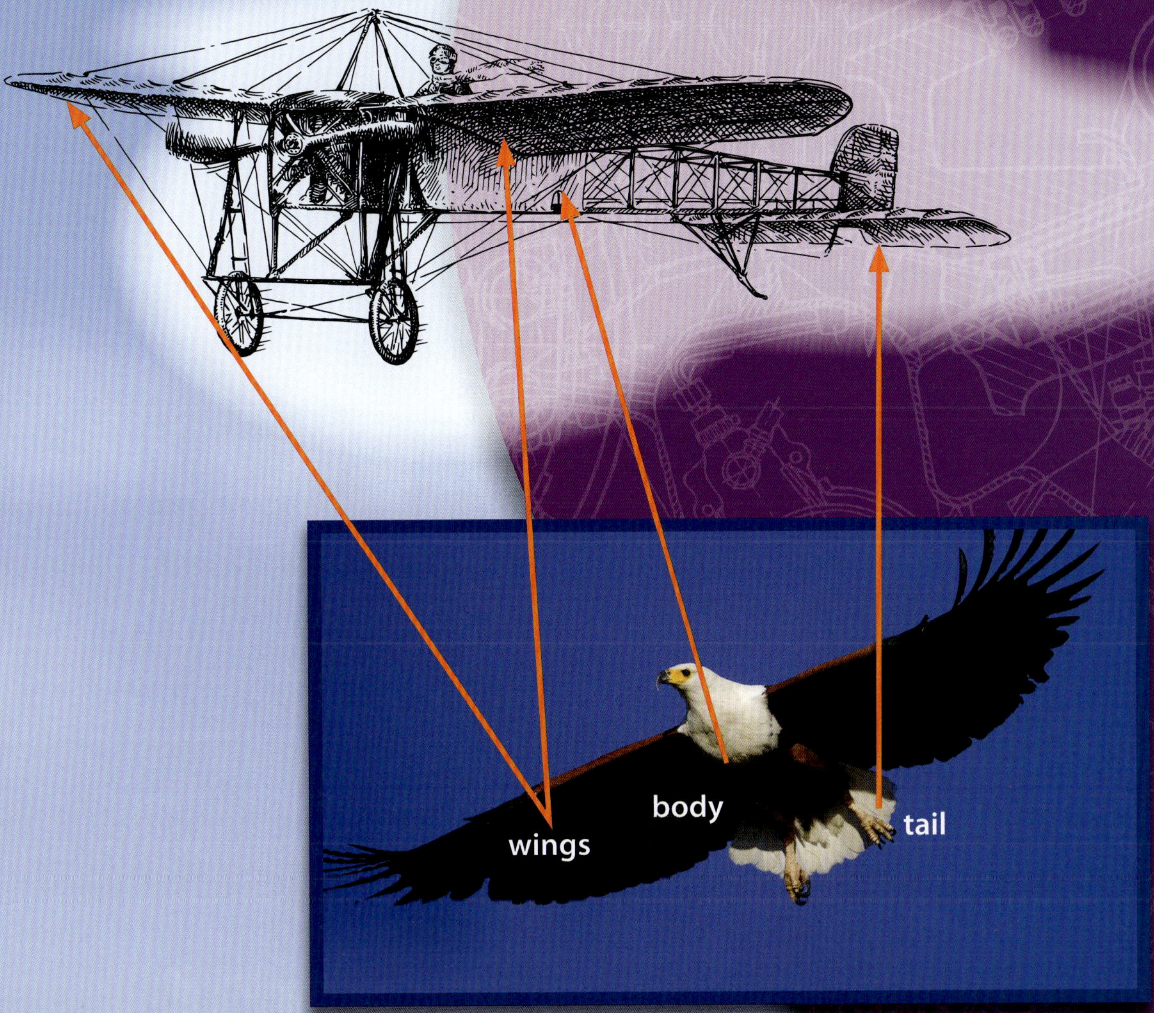

December 17, 1903

The Wright Brothers make the first flight in an airplane.

November 13, 1907

Paul Cornu is the first to fly a manned helicopter.

July 25, 1909

Louis Blériot is the first to fly across the English Channel.

The Wright Brothers

It was two brothers who finally made people's dream of flying come true. Orville and Wilbur Wright were the first to build a powered plane that could really fly. First, they had some problems to solve. They needed to make an engine's weight light enough to get off the ground. Then they had to figure out how to keep the plane in the air once it got there!

▲ Orville Wright

▲ Wilbur Wright

Who Set the Record?

Both Orville and Wilbur flew that day in 1903, each taking two turns. The fourth and longest flight, 852 feet in 59 seconds, was flown by Wilbur.

Flight Time Line

October 1909	September 1911	December 10, 1911
Elise de Laroche becomes the first female pilot.	The first airmail in the United States is delivered.	Cal Rodgers makes the first flight across a continent.

In December of 1903, Orville flew the first powered plane. He did not fly very far. And, he did not fly very high. But, he did fly! In later years, the airplane was improved. It was able to carry more people. It could also fly farther.

The First to Fly?

The Wright Brothers were not the first to soar through the air. Hot-air balloons and gliders had been flown before. The brothers were the first to fly an airplane that was powered, had a person inside it, was heavier than air, and was controllable. That was an amazing feat!

▼ Orville Wright flew the first successful manned flight in 1903.

March 1, 1912	June 15, 1921	May 9, 1926
Albert Berry makes the first parachute jump from a powered airplane.	Bessie Coleman becomes the first African-American pilot.	Richard Byrd and Floyd Bennett are the first to fly over the North Pole.

Charles Lindbergh

When planes were first used, they were only flown over land. The distance an airplane could travel had increased, but planes still were unable to fly very far away. In 1927, that all changed. A plane was flown across the ocean by a man named Charles Lindbergh (LIND-burg).

Lindbergh flew a plane from New York to Paris, France. The trip took more than 33 hours to complete.

Lucky Lindy

Lindbergh was very popular. People called him "Lucky Lindy." His fame helped to spread the word about planes and make them popular, too. Lindbergh also worked hard to improve planes and air travel.

Flight Time Line

May 20–21, 1927	June 17, 1928	May 15, 1930
Charles Lindbergh makes the first nonstop solo flight across the Atlantic Ocean.	Amelia Earhart becomes the first woman to cross the Atlantic Ocean.	Ellen Church becomes the first flight attendant.

Lindbergh made the whole trip without ever sleeping. In order to stay awake, Lindbergh put his head out the window to get a blast of cold air on his face.

When he made it to Paris, there was a big celebration. After the flight, he became a hero, and airplane travel was forever changed.

▼ Lindbergh's plane, the *Spirit of St. Louis*

Amelia Earhart

In 1928, Amelia Earhart became the first woman to fly across the Atlantic Ocean. In 1932, she flew it in a record 14 hours and 56 minutes! She died in 1937 while trying to fly around the world.

December 1, 1935
The first air traffic control center begins operating.

December 17, 1935
A successful **passenger** airliner takes off for the first time.

1936
The first **pressurized** cabin plane is built.

Commercial Flight

The **military** was the first group to use planes widely. Some planes were used in World War I. But, they were mostly used in World War II.

The World Wars

World War I (1914 to 1918) and World War II (1939 to 1945) were fought among many countries of the world. Planes played a large role in both wars. Because of planes, bullets were fired and bombs were dropped from the skies.

Flight Time Line

1939	September 18, 1947	October 14, 1947
The first jet plane is flown.	The United States Air Force is established.	Charles Yeager is the first to fly faster than the speed of sound.

After World War II, many planes were not being used. So, they were used for **commercial** (kuh-MUR-shuhl) reasons. People began to travel by plane for long distances instead of taking trains.

By the 1950s, planes were very popular. They were used for long-distance travel more than any other kind of transportation.

▼ boarding a plane

▼ inside an airplane in the 1950s

March 2, 1949	1958	1969
The first nonstop flight around the world is made.	The Federal Aviation Agency is created.	The first manned spaceship is flown to and lands on the moon.

How Planes Work

Have you ever wondered how such a big machine can get off the ground? It really is amazing. The answer is **aerodynamics** (AIR-oh-die-NAM-iks).

First, an airplane must have a powerful engine. This **thrusts** it forward. Next, there must be enough force to push up the plane.

▲ Using the four forces shown in the diagram above, a plane takes off.

▲ An airplane can take off on water as well as on land. Lift keeps the plane in the air.

Have you ever put your hand out the window of a moving car? Think about how the air pushed your hand upward. That is the force called **drag**.

Finally, the wings change the drag into a force called **lift**. They do this with their shape and angle. This keeps the plane in the air.

Parts of a Plane

An airplane has many parts to help it fly. The body of the plane is called the **fuselage** (FYOO-suh-LAHZH). This is where the pilot and passengers sit. The **wings** are used to control the plane and keep it level.

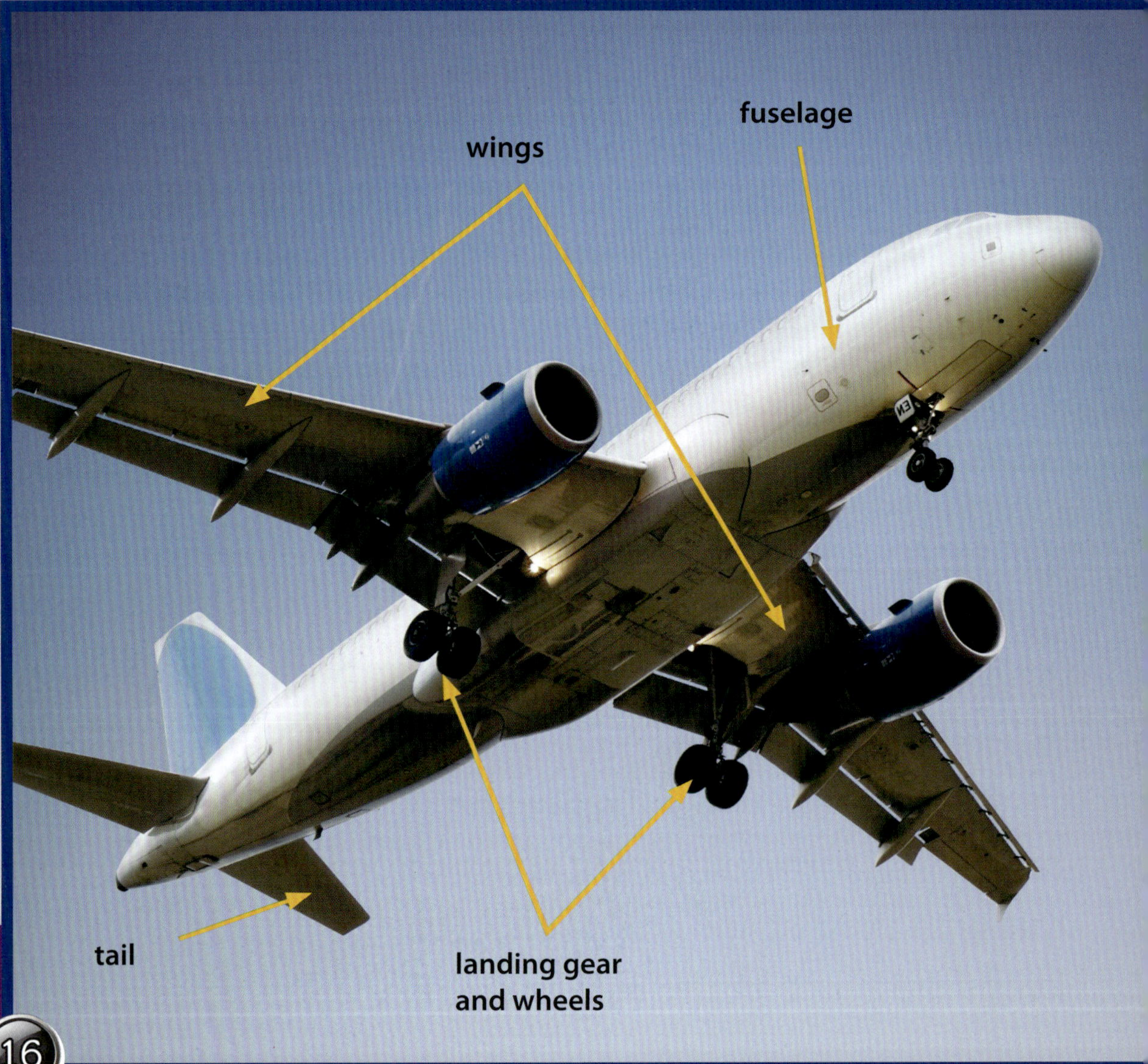

The wings help lift the plane off the ground. The **tail** helps the plane go up and down and turn direction. **Landing gear** is under the body of the plane. When the plane lands, wheels drop down from the body. The wheels allow the plane to make a gentle landing.

▲ After the sun sets, pilots use the runway lights to land the plane.

▼ landing gear and wheels

Some airplanes use **propellers**. Propellers spin like fans. They are powered by the plane's engine.

Other planes use **jet engines**. The jet engine uses **fuel** and air to move the plane. This kind of engine is powerful. It makes the plane travel fast.

Over the years, plane designs have changed. The wings have been moved to different positions. Because of this, the airplane can take off on a shorter **runway**.

▼ propeller plane

▲ jet plane

▲ jet engine

The Interior of a Plane

The interior of the plane is made up of many parts. The diagram below shows the various parts of a plane's interior.

The Interior

The inside where the passengers sit is called the main **cabin**. During the flight, passengers and crew members can use the **lavatory**. That is what a bathroom is called on a plane. The pilot and co-pilot sit in the **cockpit**.

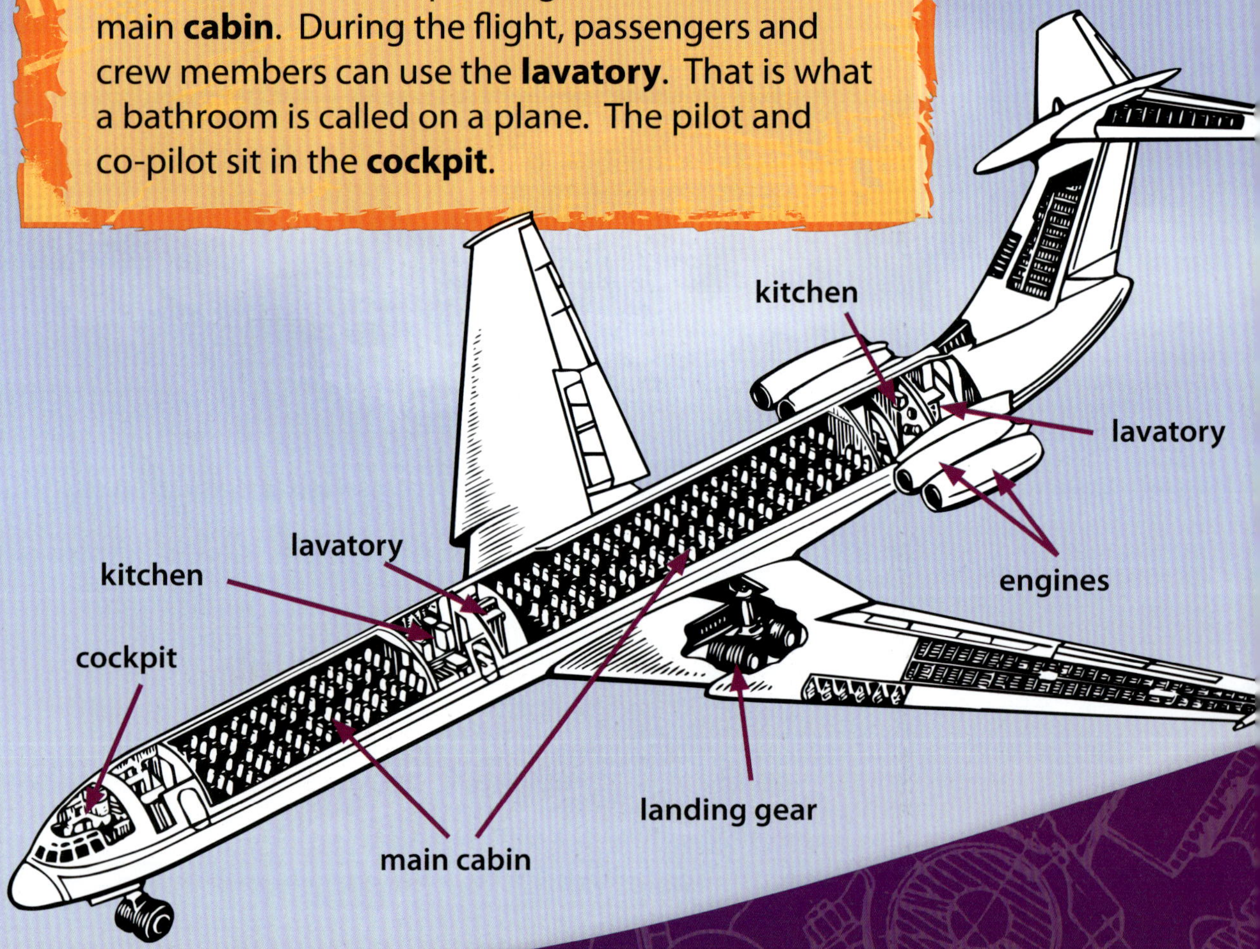

▲ inside the cockpit

◀ As passengers board on one side of the plane, the luggage is loaded into the belly of the plane.

Pressurized Cabins

In earlier years, planes could not fly any higher than 10,000 feet. If planes went higher, people inside became dizzy and sometimes fainted. The higher a plane goes, the less air there is. Less air means less **oxygen** for people to breathe.

But pilots wanted to avoid storms by flying above them. Storms make flights very bumpy. This rough travel causes some passengers to get sick. So, planes were built to solve this problem.

▼ inside an airplane cabin

Today, the inside of a plane is pressurized. That means air is pumped into the cabin. There is plenty of oxygen now. Airplanes can fly much higher, and passengers are much happier!

Pack Smart!

The airport is responsible for every bag and suitcase that goes on the plane. With nearly 1 billion flights each year, that is a lot of baggage! Make sure your suitcase is secure and follows these guidelines:

- Check the latest list of items that are allowed on the plane.
- Pack light. Do not bring more than you need. You will be glad when you are carrying your bags.
- Do not pack any fragile or very expensive items. If you must bring these items, carry them on the plane with you. Do not put them in a suitcase.
- Do not pack laptops or other electronics.
- Do not pack food or drink items. You can bring a snack on the plane, but food in your suitcase can get very messy.

Airplane Safety

Safety is the top priority of pilots and flight attendants. They spend many hours training to keep passengers safe. They practice how to deal with stormy weather or technical trouble.

Turbulence

Turbulence is felt as planes travel through the air. It can feel like a bumpy ride on an unpaved street or like a roller coaster. It's not usually dangerous, but it's important to keep your seat belt on when you are flying. Turbulence can happen suddenly and unexpectedly. Your seat belt will keep you safe when the plane runs into turbulence.

Safety First!

Passengers play an important role in safety, too. Follow these guidelines when you fly to make your flight as safe as possible.

- Listen carefully to any instructions from the pilot or flight attendants, and always wear your seat belt.
- Look for exits and make sure there is a clear path if it's necessary to leave the plane quickly.
- Turn off cell phones, computers, music players, and other electronic devices during takeoff. They can interfere with the plane's equipment.

Plane Transportation

Air travel has made life easier for most people. We can fly to faraway places in a short time. We take plane trips to visit family and friends and to go on vacations. Many people take planes regularly for business trips. Mail often travels by plane. Airplanes have become bigger, faster, and safer. They can travel day or night to almost anywhere in the world.

Glossary

aerodynamics—the study of objects moving through the air

cabin—the area inside an airplane where the passengers ride

cockpit—where the pilot and co-pilot sit on a plane

commercial—used to make money; used to move goods

drag—the force created when an object pushes against air

fuel—something that is burned to make energy

fuselage—the body of an airplane

jet engine—a powerful engine that releases gases under pressure from the rear vent of a plane to move it

landing gear—the wheels and shock absorbing equipment below a plane

lavatory—the bathroom on a plane

lift—the force, created by wings, that keeps a plane in the air

military—the soldiers and protectors of a country

model—a plan for something to be built

oxygen—a gas that has no color or taste, needed by people to breathe

passenger—someone who travels in a plane or other type of transportation

pressurized—sealed so that normal air, including oxygen, can be pumped inside and not escape

propellers—blades, like a fan, used to provide thrust to move airplanes or boats

runway—a special road used by planes for taking off and landing

tail—the back end of a plane that helps it to fly smoothly and keep steady in the air

thrust—forcing something forward

wings—the parts of a plane used to lift it off the ground and keep it level

Index